Store Math

Dawn James

Cavendish
Square

New York

Published in 2015 by Cavendish Square Publishing, LLC
243 5th Avenue, Suite 136, New York, NY 10016

Website: cavendishsq.com

This publication represents the opinions and views of the author based on his or her personal experience, knowledge, and research. The information in this book serves as a general guide only. The author and publisher have used their best efforts in preparing this book and disclaim liability rising directly or indirectly from the use and application of this book.

CPSIA Compliance Information: Batch #WW15CSQ

All websites were available and accurate when this book was sent to press.

Library of Congress Cataloging-in-Publication Data

James, Dawn, author.
Store math / Dawn James.
pages cm. — (Math around us)
Includes index.
ISBN 978-1-50260-162-9 (hardcover) ISBN 978-1-50260-165-0 (paperback) ISBN 978-1-50260-169-8 (ebook)
1. Counting—Juvenile literature. 2. Arithmetic—Juvenile literature. 3. Shopping—Juvenile literature. I. Title.

QA113.J373 2015
513.2—dc23

2014032628

Editor: Amy Hayes
Copy Editor: Cynthia Roby
Art Director: Jeffrey Talbot
Designer: Douglas Brooks
Senior Production Manager: Jennifer Ryder-Talbot
Production Editor: David McNamara
Photo Researcher: J8 Media

The photographs in this book are used by permission and through the courtesy of: Cover photo by DAJ/Getty Images; sonyae/iStock/Thinkstock, 5; Blend Images - Noel Hendrickson/Brand X Pictures/Getty Images, 7; Juice Images/Cultura/Getty Images, 9; Don Bayley/iStock/Thinkstock, 11; kali9/E+/Getty Images, 13; Blend Images/John Lund/Marc Romanelli/Blend Images/Getty Images, 15; Cathy Yeulet/Hemera/Thinkstock, 17; Andresr/Shutterstock.com, 19; Jade/Blend Images/Getty Images, 21.

Printed in the United States of America

Contents

We go shopping at the store.

How many **cucumbers** is James holding?

James is holding **2** cucumbers.

Milk is important to buy at the store.

How many jugs of milk does Annika have?

She has **1** jug.

Gina picks up **2 pineapples**.

Her mom tells her to put **1** back.

How many pineapples are left?

1 pineapple is left.

We need eggs for **breakfast**.

How many eggs are in the **carton**?

6 eggs are in the carton.

11

Now it's time to get a treat!

Lauren picks out **2** chocolate cupcakes and **1** vanilla cupcake.

How many cupcakes did she get?

She got **3** cupcakes.

13

Liz needs some shirts.

She picks out a blue shirt and a green shirt.

How many shirts does she pick out?

She picks out **2** shirts.

15

This store has many **aisles**.

Cynthia and her dad walk down **8** aisles, then they walk down **2** more.

How many aisles have they walked down?

They have walked down **10** aisles.

It's time to check out.

Amy's family buys apples, bananas, and oranges.

How many types of fruit do they buy?

They buy **3** types.

18

19

Shirley and her mom pack up the car.

How many bags do they have?

They have **2** bags.

It was a great day at the store.

New Words

aisles (EYELZ) Areas where people walk through stores.

breakfast (BREK-fast) The first meal of the day, eaten in the morning.

carton (CAR-ton) A container made of cardboard or plastic.

cucumbers (CUE-cum-berz) Green vegetables that have many seeds.

pineapples (PYN-a-plz) Sweet, tropical fruits that are yellow on the inside.

Index

About the Author

Dawn James loves taking photographs and going to baseball games. She lives in Pittsburgh, Pennsylvania.

About

Bookworms help independent readers gain reading confidence through high-frequency words, simple sentences, and strong picture/text support. Each book explores a concept that helps children relate what they read to the world they live in.